FROM AN ACACIA LANDSCAPE

Abdirahman Mirreh

Poetry 1983-93

HAAN

Published by HAAṆ Publishing
PO Box 607, London SW16 1EB

ISBN 1 874209 86 3

Typeset in Berkeley

Printed in Great Britain by
The Ipswich Book Company Ltd, Ipswich, Suffolk.

Cover design and page layout: David Bird
Cover photo by Anita Adam
Pictures on pp 18, 38, and 68/69 by the Author

CONTENTS

DEDICATION

To the Somali National Movement's fighters who died on the battlefield - in the rural areas, the towns, and the villages of Somaliland - fighting against the brutal military dictatorship of Siad Barre.

To the SNM members who died natural deaths after years of struggle.

To those who were maimed during the liberation war and to those who were tortured during the rule of Siad Barre.

To the pastoralists and civilians who not only fought side by side with the SNM liberation forces, but who sacrificed their animals and properties for the just cause. To the pastoralists and civilians who were raped, robbed and killed.

It is impossible for me to name here the thousands of Mujahadin fighters who died during the liberation war of Somaliland. For this reason I mention only those I met or whose names I became acquainted with through surviving SNM members. For those whose names are not mentioned, it is not my intention to omit them - the whole are represented by the few herewith named.

Maxamed Cali
Cali Tuur Maxamed Warsame
Maxamed Xaashi Lixle
Xuseen Kharash Yare
Xandule
Mahdi Cali
Xuseen Xannaan
Haragwaafi
Cabdillahi Cuddo
Xasan Saleebaan
Cabdillahi Saciid
Ibraahin Haliqin
Cabdi Xaashi
Maxamed Ibraahin (Weerer)
Cabdilqaadir Koosaar
Aadan Sheikh Cabdi (Shiine)
Aadan Saleebaan
Ibraahin Koodbuur Axmed
Axmed Macalin Haruun

Ismaaciil Xaagi Cabdi
Talyaani
Cabdi Muxumed Feyr
Ibraahim X. Ileeye
Gacmadheere
Saleebaan A. Qalabjaan
Maxamed Mooge
Bidhiidh
Jaamac Yare
Saleebaan Elmi (Baylood)
Maxamed Haybe
Caydiid Jaamac (Sacuudi)
Cabdi Cumar Hadrawi
Cumar Cali Dhuux
Cabdi I. Mire (Darawal)
Bidixo
Cabdi Abiid Cismaan
Maxamed Guhaad Cabdi
Maxamed Saalax Nuur
Cabdraxamaan (Juxo)
Yuusuf J. Bulaale (Madaxdiin)
Cabdinaasir
Guutaale
Bacaw

ACKNOWLEDGEMENTS

I would like very much to express my thanks and profound gratitude to the following women and men who, in one way or another, helped me after I fled the civil war in what was then the northern part of Somalia, but which since May 1991 has been the Somaliland Republic:
P. Daemisch, Prof. F. Barth, Dr.R.Bauer, Dr.R.Neudexk, Dr. I.Kappel, M.I.Yassin 'Colaad', Farah H. Hussein, Abdirahman J. M. Mirreh, Abdirahman M. Handulleh, Col. M. Kahin, Dr. Bidhiidh, Prof. H. Eidheim, Marie T. Lanz, and Dr. M. Warsame; the Norwegian Government and the Norwegian people.

Abdirahman G. Mirreh
Oslo, 1996

A Ramadan Evening -
Lover and Father

I carried garlic, onions, lemons
and all the tropical fruits you loved.

I tiptoed and reached
your house. I knocked on the window
and saw your shadow moving in the room.

My heart began to beat heavily
my legs suddenly trembled
I heard coughing.

I dropped the basket with all
its contents
then the coughing was familiar
why didn't you tell me he would be
at home?

I gathered my strength and ran
like a coward from a battlefield.
I jumped over the cactus fence
higher than a galloping horse

And before I landed I remembered
what you said . . . He will be
at the mosque breaking
the fast.

HARGEISA 1983

Four Horses and a Wadi

The Gu' rain arrived.
The drops were not heavy
the air was cold, the breeze light
yet the hair on my arms rose.

And slowly the wadi flowed
no logs were floating
no froth was carried.

Four horses grazed on its bank
testing the current
with their lips; ah! fear . . .

How could they know
A wadi's unusual flow?

HARGEISA/GEED XAABEEYE,
MAY 1988

Memories of Life and Death

Nursing memories
of more than two decades
upon the soil where they once
blossomed and slowly
breathed the air and grew
before death embraced them,

Now walking on the very grass
where they were born
I asked myself
should I let them rest
or should I let them blossom again?

OSLO 20.5.93

Death of a Sheikh

In a town called Harar
in the east of Ethiopia
there lived a man
by the name of Derba Sheikh.

He fed hyenas from his hand
his fingers touched their mighty
teeth yet they never bit his hand.
How could they? It fed them.

He fed them every night
in a queue patiently they stood
more than humans would do
all this happened while the townsfolk slept.

And when he died two workers
from the municipality carried
him to his grave
the ceremony was brief
the burial was quick.

The municipality men returned
they reached the market square
they shouted loud toward the east
toward the west - the hyena-man is dead!

A mullah said he was a jin
another shouted he was a hyena
and in the end an old lady
said he was a saint.

And before the dawn greeted the land
all his friends gathered
and sat beside his grave
mourning in their way.

Silence had fallen on the air
painful was their departure
they could hardly walk
towards the Balaadh plain.

HARAR/HARGEISA/OSLO 6.93

Once there was a Tasmanian
For Bosnia

No trials took place
as the white man wiped out
the Tasmanian race.

No woman, no man is left.
Nowhere on this earth
can we admire their beautiful faces

Not much is written about their fate
no one is left that we can save.

Their culture is forever lost
the last person carried it to his grave.

We can trace his ancestors' skulls.
The white man is responsible
for the extermination of his race.

OSLO 6.6.93

Unwanted Plant

Although no one likes to have it
in his garden or on his farm

Yet many enjoy the beauty
of the dandelion in the Spring.

OSLO 16.6.93

The Fuhrer's Ghost

1939 it started with the Jews
1993 it is starting with the Turks
the Slavs are the next
the bomb for the rest.

OSLO 17.6.93

For B. Backer

I never cried, not that I remember,
it is not in my culture
it is against my pride.

Yet when I heard you had died
the tears ran down my cheeks
and when I recovered from the shock
I realised my shirt was soaked.

OSLO 17.6.93

Profound Pain
To A.M. Warsame

Someone you loved dearly
all of a sudden gone;
childhood memories circulating
in your head

Remembering places;
the bushes where you played
hide and seek;
the gardens along the wadi
where you stole lemons and grapes.

To whom shall I complain?
To the Gu' rain?
To the antelope grazing
on the Qoolcadey plain?

No, no - with no one shall I share
my profound pain.

OSLO 12.7.93

Untitled

After a long journey through the night
dawn, tired, has at last arrived;
the crow awakes, shakes his wings
and calls the Moslems to their morning prayer

And before they hear the voice
of the muezzin, before he utters the words
Allah is great!   I can imagine the men
streaming in haste to the mosque.

And on their way some gaze at the women
balancing baskets on their heads,
swinging their hips left and right,
but others cast their eyes to the ground
avoiding the swing lest Satan . . .

I, lying in my bed and hearing the first amen
before the first kneeling to the floor,
decide with a bad conscience to enjoy
the warmth of my bed.

OSLO 12.7.93

Distance

Where the desert kisses
the horizon,
and the dawn embraces
the end of the world

Where both meet eternity
in the twilight, and evening stars
conduct the orchestra, each taking
his turn, until dawn disturbs the festivity,

Where melodies and music
are always alive, yet few hear them,
where the rainbow colours blossom
and die

There, quietly, very quietly,
I pour out my sorrows pail after pail,
without complaint, without a soul
hearing me.

OSLO 12.7.93

Listen or Do Not Listen

And I shall write another poem
on the pages of the dawn

And if no one understands it,
the monsoon
and the acacia leaves will.

They will read it to the dew, while
resting on the grass before sunrise,
before it descends to the ground.

OSLO 9.8.93

Roots and Democracy
To Nazim Hikmet

The east is dead
the west still breathing
democracy we had
before the white man
came.

Before he arrived
on our shores
no jails we had
nor police posts
not even an army
that led men to war.

To settle a dispute
persuasion was the
rule.

And now ... ?

OSLO 1993

Ungrateful - A Daughter in Europe

The cock sat on the eggs
until they hatched
he fed them with the best
corn of the land
until they grew.

Now they are
beautiful and strong
they laugh at him
because he is old
they ask him why he is
bald.

OSLO 11.11.92

Passage to Nowhere - Life after Death
To S and A

In a fairy tale they met
in the land of God
in the land of the Prophet
in the heart of the desert.

Memories of yesterday
cannot be taken away.

The beauty of her face
is rare.   God has bestowed
upon her more beauty
than the Queen
of Sheba.

In their country again
they met, under the acacia
shade their eyes met.
His were sending a message,
of hers he was not sure.

He left the country
and returned again
Ah! . . . He did not dare
to ask where she lived.

A decade passed, at last
they met . . . a telephone.
He sighed . . . and
wished to be there,
to lay down his heart,
accompanied with
flowers, on her doorstep
and if not now perhaps
after death.

OSLO/HARGEISA 1986/1992

A Galool Tree Named Desire

Empty streets, once flanked
by whitewashed houses
that now lay side by side,
some completely ruined
others half-destroyed
standing like monuments
erected centuries ago.

I didn't meet the pariah
dogs that once roamed
these streets, nor could
I hear their barking
from the vicinity of
the abattoir.

No longer do the women
sell a glass of tea under
the acacia trees.

How did it happen? Once a
beautiful place
now a ghost-town -
this is what I thought
as I walked in the
heat of noon.

And as my feet rested
on a fallen stone,
I stood for a moment
inhaling the scent
from a tree . . .

I remembered a galool
tree that stands at the
edge of the Tuyo plain
an old man named
desire.   HARGEISA/OSLO 31.5.92

17

A Virus Named Progress

As a child henna
was my shampoo
the leaf of a qasil tree
was my soap.

I cleaned the cooking
pot with sand
a very white sand.

Ajax was there
in the shops, my mother
wouldn't buy it, the smell.

My toothpaste was
from the adey shrub
I combed my hair with
a wooden comb.

And now my children
want shampoo
perfumed soap
and toothpaste
with a chemical taste.

OSLO 18.7.92

Just a Piece of Bread

Oh Moon! you illuminate
the world
you are not there
to warm it

Your brightness guided
the caravans through the desert
and the dhows on the seas
through all the centuries.

Man has landed on you -
how much money he spent
to let his feet touch your soil! -
yet there is a child on our earth
screaming in the night
for a piece of bread.

OSLO 23.10.92

Africa

Is your destiny
tied only to wars?
Must your children
grow under falling bombs?
Must they carry guns
at the age of ten?

Must they grow under the banner
of fear and hate? Must their
brains be painted with pictures
of horror and death?

Must they judge life
only with the barrel of the gun?
Africa, must the white man
enslave you and rule again?

OSLO 23.11.92

The Moon and the Melon

Walking on the strand
where Oslo fjord ends

I gazed at the moon.
Half full she was -
the shape of
a watermelon sliced
in two

Melon so sweet, sweeter
than sugar cane - ah!
childhood memories

Remembering Mohamed Warsame's
farm where he raised
turkeys and grew
citrus fruit.

OSLO 16.12.92

The Golden Bowl

Once our golden
bowl was filled
with flowers and love

But now in my heart
weeds have sprouted.
The undergrowth
is wider than an
untended field

And before the cock
brought the message
to the land, I looked
at your beautiful face
while you were fast
asleep; I didn't dare
to touch you.

OSLO 24.12.92

Yearning

A nomad son doesn't
know his age but he
knows the seasons
of the rain.

He has no permanent
abode, nor bills to pay.
He loads his camels
and moves to new
pasture and fresh
water-wells.

How often do I wish
to lead his life and
leave all the comfort
I have now.

OSLO 24.12.92

24

Suffering Grass

Destiny blows like a fire
kindled by the wind,
it might protect, or it might
burn universal life.

The wind never stops rolling
the clouds in heaven
that coil themselves up
and refuse to act.

Through the mist of life
soaked in the morning dew,
the grass turns pale
as the monsoon wind,
merciless, lashes it
with the season's whip.

The grass suffers silently
it has no tears to shed
no sobbing can be heard.
Death must have its daily
prey, be it grass, man or beast.

How could it escape when the roots
were anchored in the soil centuries ago?

DUL CAD, A REFUGEE CAMP, 5.4.91

The Abattoir

To Hassan

Over the slaughterhouse
the marabou rises and descends;
marabou life is nothing to envy.

Men and women are skinning
the animals. The watch
on my wrist reads
a quarter to six -
soon the skins and hides
will be spread to dry
in the sun, and late in the afternoon
the eagles will land before
the marabou leaves.

And in the end Hassan,
the cleaner of the house,
will collect the hides and
skins, put them in
store and leave for
home carrying a leg
or some other piece of meat to
his waiting wife.

DIRE DAWA 5.5.91

A Northern Man
To Mohammed Ali

And when we met in Burao
in the year of 1988, as
we talked and argued his
words came from
the depth of the truth.

No epitaph is on his grave
a sura was read as we
buried him on a plain.

He was the one who ignited
the whole
he was a spark that
set the forest aflame

And he died on the battlefield
standing firm on his heels.
We carried him silently
with slow steps with no
regret or sorrow
on the litter
to his grave,
and we saw the sun
shed tears in the colour
of its beams.

ADDIS ABEBA 8.5.91

The Answer
To Bob Dylan

I remember the Gu' rain
and all the acacia names,
I remember June and September
as the bullets twisted in the air.

I remember the words
of a song . . . but the answer
doesn't lie in the wind
my friend.

HARGEISA/OSLO 13.6.91

Mutual Trade

The truth is we never learned
a single thing from the First
and the Second War.

The truth is we never learned
from Vietnam
and now there are hundreds
of forgotten wars
in Africa and Latin America,
in Asia too.

The question is who
buys the coffee beans,
who gives the generals
the poison gas, the armoured cars?

HARGEISA/OSLO 13.6.91

Children's Game, Hargeisa

I hear the Americans
will rebuild the town,
a town their guns completely
destroyed and levelled to the ground.

It reminds me of a child
I saw on a holiday beach
playing on the sand,
building castles and
after a while destroying
them again.

OSLO 12.7.91

Progress

No more do the nomads travel
through the land on foot
no, now they travel
with trucks.

No more do they load
the corn on a camel's
back, they travel
with trucks.
Toyota and Nissan
they hire for the
Haud.

The grass doesn't grow -
the water follows
the tyre tracks.
The drought is
longer - the sheep
are suffering.

But it is not the
weather.

OSLO 12.7.91

Ghost City - Hargeisa

The hills released the first breeze
of the season,
the morning flowers' scent
was lingering in the air.
I tried to touch the morning
by its mane
alas! it escaped.
I was a living soul in a ghost city
in search of what I could find.

OSLO 15.7.91

Remembering the Marabou

The rain ceased without warning
the rainbow didn't kiss
your lips nor mine.
You were there walking
by my side
but long ago you left.

It was yesterday that
we walked along
the lake, threw
stones at the marabou
and chased
the butterfly, laughing.

You fell and I followed
you to the ground
and you were like
a lotus.

OSLO 17.7.91

The Galool Tree and Acid Rain

The morning enveloped
in the realm of the night
opened its buds before
sunrise
like a rose born
from the embryo of
the Spring.
The bees diligently
buzzed in the air
kissing the flowers
here and there.
I lay the whole day
on the earth, in God's
nature, between the
galool and the gob trees,
watching the creations
of God.
And before the lights
of the setting sun
disappeared beyond the
horizon
no pigeons were
in the sky,
only three eagles
were flying home.
And I wondered, wondered
and wondered endlessly
how many years it
will take until the acid
rain reaches these trees.

OSLO 19.7.91

Beyond the Great Water

I didn't vow to remain
nor never to venture
beyond my native shore.

And yet with all the comfort
I now enjoy,
one wish I have -
one moment or two
to sit under the shade
of a galool tree to enjoy
the afternoon breeze.

I do not regret that
I have left.
Ah! The unknown lures
and that is . . .

OSLO 21.7.91

Addiction

Like a teacher whose
addiction is flogging
some women's addiction
is simply nagging.

OSLO 23.5.91

Untitled

I do think sometimes
what is this life?
What is it all about
if one will end in a dark,
damp, cold grave?

OSLO 23.7.91

False Claim

The Kingdom of Saudi Arabia
is a Moslem land
'It is the guardian
of the Islamic shrine'.

Moslem refugees are being killed
day after day
by bullets, hunger and disease.

Yet Saudi's billions are lying in America's banks,
the Emirs are enjoying champagne and
women in their villas in Egypt and Spain.
Christian countries are pouring tents, food,
medicine and household goods
into the Moslem refugee camps.

Yet the Kingdom's rulers claim
to be the guardians of the Moslem shrine,
the three Moslem houses of God.
What a paradox - what a lie
to God, to the whole world
to the Moslem world!

HARTA SHEIKH, A REFUGEE CAMP/
OSLO 8.91

A Hell of a Road

Imagine the road -
the length and breadth I trailed,
how far could it spread?

How many miles will it stretch
from a nomad hut to a PhD?
And in the end I asked myself
what did I really
gain in this world?

Wouldn't I be better
if I herded my father's camels
on the Tuyo plain?

OSLO 1.8.91

At the Well

We were alone at the well
you drew water and I stood
hours watching you
our lips didn't meet
yet our shadows embraced.

Evening clouds sailed
towards the setting sun
I spent the night
at the well waiting for you

And as the dawn unfolded
with all the light it possessed
I left the beauty of our ancestral land
where we were born

I left the hills, the steppe, the Qotton plain
where our fathers with their herds
freely roamed.
I left for the industrial world
and what did I gain?

OSLO 2.8.91

Remembering the Ugly General

They tell me, do not
be rebellious, African man!
I say why shouldn't I?

You give the general all the aid
but nothing reaches the poor man
why on earth shouldn't I be a rebellious
man?

With the guns you give to the general
I shall strengthen my rebellion
when I take the guns you give
to the general.

These guns of yours are daily
used to kill my folk.
I shall be rebellious - if it's not
possible with guns, then with words,
with the brain and tongue God
bestowed upon me
with the ink and the pen I possess.

I shall be rebellious
even if I could move
only one finger before my
death.

I shall be rebellious
in my grave
as long as injustice
in this world prevails.

ADDIS ABEBA/OSLO 6.6.91/6.8.91

Trees

Beneath a blue Norwegian sky,
hills with trees
surrounding villages and towns.

Walking in a forest
among the birches and the pines -
yet I miss the dixi-grass
and the acacia trees.

OSLO 11.8.91

Mr. President!
To the Presidents of the Industrial World

Mr. President!
The 'third world' needs
not cannons and bullets
but, desperately, bread.

We know you have great factories
we know they produce arsenals.

Mr. President!
Why do you never check
where your 'humanitarian aid',
the weapons you give to the friendly generals,
really go,
against whom they are used?

Mr. President!
How could you speak
of democracy, when the guns you
give to the generals are used
against children
like your own?

HARGEISA/OSLO 14.8.91

Disappointment

Sitting on an island rock
in the Norwegian fjord
I watched with folded arms
the autumn waves in ebb and flow.

The sun was setting,
in the west a boat
with a family sailing home.

And in my day-dream
three seagulls visited the spot,
they thought I had a piece of bread,
perhaps two,
but, poor birds, I had
to disappoint them.

Darkness fell - my skin felt
the autumn evening breeze.
The ferry came.

HOVEDOYA-OSLO 15.8.91

Strength of Will

What strength
nature bestowed
upon a delicate seed!

How could it break
through the ribs and
veins of such massive rocks?

OSLO 24.10.91

The White Man

First you came
with the Bible,
mirrors, beads.

You built churches
with my forest wood,
stone and my sweat.

Then you forbade me
to worship my gods
or visit my ancestors' shrines.

And as the years
passed by you chained me
and took me over the
great water.

You raped my mother,
sister and daughter,
you separated my family.

You sold each one of us
to a new 'master'
and when I rebelled
against your brutality
you hanged me from a tree
lashed my body with a whip
until my flesh was torn,
until my blood soaked the soil.

You colonised my motherland,
you took all the statues
I had moulded in bronze
then you told me I had no culture.
But you exhibited my achievement
in your museums - how was this?

You stole the wealth
beneath my earth
diamonds, gold, silver
and all the rest
God gave me.

And in the end I freed
myself from the chains
yet you kept the
richness of my land
and the means of my
livelihood in your hands.

The prices of my products
are determined in your
capitals and I come like
a beggar asking for 'aid'.

The projects you made
you imposed on me
the money flowed back to
your banks, to the general's
personal account.

You knew it, and now
I am in debt up to the neck
your projects failed
because they were fake.

You gave the general
all the arms he asked for
he didn't protect
the borders of my land with them
but killed instead
those who dared to oppose his rule.

I am the only member of
a family of ten
lucky enough to escape
the general's war.
Sick and frail I reached
the gate of your city.

At last, I thought,
I had reached the haven
of peace and democracy.
Alas! racism is haunting
me on your streets,
buses and trains.

The looks and the
insulting words - don't
you feel ashamed?
If I were you I would have
buried my face in the
sand . . .

OSLO 9.11.91

January Wind

Oh God! how I enjoy
the wind
the swinging twigs
of the birch tree

Oh God! how I enjoy
the wind
like a rajah riding
his best elephant
in the land of Sind.

OSLO 29.1.90

Soft Falling Flakes

Oh God! how I enjoy
walking
on the snow.

Oh God! how I
enjoy the flakes
descending on my
face.

Ah! not a single
croak of the frog
from the pond

Oh! where is
the ugly cry
of the crow?

OSLO JANUARY 1990

The Glory of Death

Destiny blows in the
direction it wills.
The mind never stops
rolling.
Clouds can coil themselves
up in heaven and
refuse to act.

Through the mist
of life, soaked in
the morning dew,
the grass turns
pale as it is lashed
by the monsoon,
the season's whip,
and although at the
end it weakens and
blows gently, yet the
poor grass suffers
silently.

No tears it sheds,
no sobbing can be
heard and like any other
unknown hero it meets
death with glory.

OSLO 1.3.90

Countryside Stroll

Where clouds conceal not
the moon
and smog pollutes no air

Where evening stars
parade punctually
in certain lines of the sky
each in its place -
I often asked
about mine
as I gazed at the sky

The question is unanswered
but the twinkle
soothed me.

OSLO 6.3.90

Autumn Wind

You carry the
falling leaves
you smash them
against the walls.

From faraway acres
you blow the particles
of soil to places they
have never seen.

You make me feel
your anger and your
tenderness, yet offered
so far this one single
poem.

Should we remain
together - should we
remain friends?

Should we seek divorce
through nature's court?
Should the birch be
witness?

My lawyer should be the
spring, and yours I know is
the winter that brings
depressing gloom.

OSLO
SEPTEMBER 1989/MARCH 1990

Acacia Shade

I have not been long
away from home but God!
how I long for
the shade of an acacia tree.

The camels resting underneath
escape the midday heat
through which even a mad dog
or Englishman could
hardly stroll.

And when the evening breeze
travels softly through
the land how I long
to hear the whistling
camel-boys.

OSLO 9.3.90

A Nurse After the Shift

He saw her leaving;
the corridor was long
the distance seemed eternity itself.
He didn't notice the paintings
on the hospital wall
nor heard as a patient groaned.

He stood there watching her
from behind
hoping she would turn
and wave goodnight.
Alas! she turned the corner
and disappeared into the night.
He could not lift his feet
and walk away - his feet were
nailed to the ground.

At last he could move,
went into his room
threw himself on his bed and
pulled the blanket hastily over
his head.

ULLVÜL SYKEHUS/OSLO 10.5.93

A Wish for a Walk

In the winter
months in a
country where the
streets are jammed
with snow

And no one cares
if someone falls
and breaks his leg
or even his neck . . .
one just closes one's eyes
and keeps
the rhythm and goes on.

And when spring
washes away the rest
of the season's snow
how grateful I am
for an evening stroll.

OSLO 14.3.90

Two Seasons and I

Two seasons -
nature parts them
and you hear
the separations crack.
Now I know
the very moment when
the next season will
really start.

But the season that
should leave refuses
to depart
and now I feel
only longing for
the one that
has to go.

OSLO 17.3.90

Whitewashed Houses

What a pleasure to be
in such a whitewashed city
watching the fishermen
mending the nets.

I stand at the quay from
where the Vikings rowed
their boats through morning
mist.

What a beautiful rainy day -
sitting in a bus
after sunset, the mountains
on the left, the fjords on
the right.

Here comes the spring,
a few days early, to touch
the trees, to awaken the
flower seeds beneath
the earth!

RISOR 2.4.90

Alienated Ramadan

In the land of God
where church bells
ring

Where words of Jesus
on Sunday are
preached

In the land of God
where man speaks
on behalf of His name

The muezzin has no minaret
to call aloud
Allah is Great.

OSLO 6.4.90

A Secret Exposed

I am tied to the rain
to the wind and no one
can guess for how long.

They fed me, they feed me
and if the wind doesn't
chase me and the rain
doesn't knock on my
door I am dead.

And without them
I feel like an orphan
with no abode in search
of his parents who died in
a war.

OSLO 23.4.90

El Negro

If the white man
thinks he is the
day

You should think
you are the night.

How could the day
be born without
the night?

OSLO 27.4.90

A Very Short Story

He came from the storm
in search of a shelter
at last he found one
with protective walls,
warmth and a solid roof.

And as the walls started
to crack he left the house
before the roof fell
in.

OSLO 27.5.92

Lonely Old Lady

Upon a barren hill
to the south of Hargeisa town
there once stood
a village full of life

Now it is deserted,
lanes decayed,
mud walls, one broken
another smeared with blood.
The whole is drenched with
innocent human
blood.

Aye . . . night,
with the sounds of a thousand
ghosts disturbing its serenity,
dead and rotten bodies scattered
all over the African bush,
the smell . . .

An old lady, the
only one left, solemnly sat
listening as a thousand acacias
wept and mourned the dead.
She gazed wearily at the sky,
watching the expressionless moon;
she sighed
in the deepest cell
of her soul and wondered
who was to blame
for the horror she saw -
was it the general
or the suppliers of the bombs?

Could this be
the wish of God?

OSLO 5.5.90

The White Caravan

The caravan arrived
carrying containers filled
with water, four gallons
apiece.

Man and beast are exhausted
after the long march
seven days and seven nights.

What a joy when all reach
the settlement safely
greeted and welcomed by
the whole hamlet!

You can hear from a distance
the grumble and gurgle
of the camels, as the women
and men unload.

And as night falls after
the cornmeal supper
the dancing starts
around the fire
not far from the
courtyard.

The moon and stars
send their blessing
down, with no bitterness
or hate - just a hamlet
full of joy until the
containers are empty again.

How I long for such a place
with a human face
full of grace!

OSLO 5.5.90

In the Small Hours of the Night

Remembering the bitter wind
echoing through the wadi
bouncing on eroded walls

The moon is fifteen days old . . .
Insomnia.

OSLO 6.5.90

The Owner of the Land

*To the Patriots of the
Somali National Movement*

Long ago - a decade or two -
the white eagles were few
the crow was left

Then came scavenging marabou
by the thousand
where did they come from?
Displacement has taken
place.

But the eagle refused to shift
even an inch from his soil
bravely he fought and ruled
his land . . .

OSLO 8.6.90

Bananas on a Tray

Tropical fruits on the stand
the buyer doesn't know how
they grew, or he doesn't care.

Sweat and blood are smeared
on the skin, yet the taste is
sweet.

A president, or a company, are
enjoying the fruits of the fruit
no one sees the stains of those
who watered it with their sweat.

OSLO 8.5.90

Wasted Time

He was uncertain if
by his efforts
he would harvest
the fast-ripening grain
or pomegranate
fruit

It was not a slow myrrh tree
he had planted,
no, he didn't
plant a coffee shrub
here and there

He did it with the care
of all his years
yet brief was his joy.
The soldiers came
and destroyed the whole.

OSLO 14.6.90

When Nomads Move

When no smoke ascends
from the hamlets,
when you can't smell fire
from a distance
in the rain

You know no tea is boiling
on the three stones of the campfire,
no fairytales are being told
to children in the evening,
nor can love be sought
in the rain.

You receive the message
with the evening breeze as you
watch the bowing leaves on
an acacia's twigs

And only then do you realise
they shifted camp in search
of grass, in search of water
for their families, for the herds
they love.

OSLO 18.6.90

Industrial World - An Eye Witness

Your guns, aeroplanes
and the speedy tanks
you sell to the general -
I think you know how they
are used, what purpose they serve

And if you don't I'll tell you now
how they are used.
I saw them used to kill children
and as they were shot, bombed and
gunned down with the arsenal
you gave the general

I saw them dying and painfully
biting the dust under the galool tree
where they used to play, which
they used to climb, among the grass
where they used to play hide and seek,
like your own children
with their friends.

And none of them knew that
the morning sun they saw
would never be seen by them
as it faded into the dusk

And no one was there within
hailing distance to hear
their screams.
I wish you were there
to see it all, to hear them.

But I was there to witness it all.

OSLO 18.6.90

Encounter Ten Years After
To Harald

Many have said praises
some have read praises

I said thank you
ten years ago
I say thank you now.

OSLO 21.6.90

The Penguin King
To Sigrun

And I asked about the penguin
poem
I wrote for her
and gave her
she couldn't find it
in her wallet among
the books

How could a poem of
such a nature
be lost
be mislaid?

And I wonder why.

OSLO 22.6.90

When Heaven Opens its Gates

Just before the small
hours enter through
the night doors

When heaven is supposed
to open its gates and
the Lord is waiting
for anyone who might
have a petition to submit,
for anyone who has a complaint
to lodge against injustice
in this world

And before I could write what
was in my heart, in my head,
trying to select the one I thought
was best, it was too late -
the door was closed.

OSLO 27.6.90

Visiting in the Night

I wonder why poems
pay me a visit while
I try to lay down my head
and sleep.

Now after decades
I know they fear
the day with its
noisy trains, trams . . .

And before the day breaks,
before the cock crows,
they ascend again to
the heavens above.

OSLO 1.7.90

Frozen Feet in Hargeisa

Hearing the hard knock
on my door
just before
the morning light
spread its blanket
over the sleeping town

In a moment of horror
I imagined in no time
the torture in my cell
and in the end, my grave

And my wife trembling
said don't open the door,
I said no you stay I'll go.

And before I had lifted my
frozen feet from the concrete
floor, I saw it was the beggar
making his morning
round.

A moment of silence ruled
the air
at last with relief the house
sighed.

OSLO 1.7.90

Waiting for Another Day

The years swallowed
down my sorrows
although they plough
the seeds of sadness
in the depth of my soul.

Yet hope never decayed
through the labyrinth
of my life, for I always
yearned for the next
daybreak.

OSLO 5.8.90

The Wretched of the Earth

The sufferers on this earth
are those who sow the
seeds in the soil but
never harvest the fruit
when it is ripe.

They labour all seasons
long with their bare
hands, you can read
the years in their wrinkled faces

You can read it on their
feet, feet that never knew
shoes, you can read it
in the depth of their souls.

No hope do they expect, the
word is unknown to them,
and not a day do they go astray
they just wait for
another dawn.

OSLO 5.8.90

Looking at Your Face

Your beautiful body and
face will decay in the soil
one day, it will
be a great feast for the ants,
for the termites.

Death is unavoidable,
you can't bribe the
angel of death, that
tears life out of your soul.

And in the end worms
will come out of your
grave, from that same once
beautiful body and face.

Ah! life . . . where did all that
beauty go?

OSLO 15.8.90

Fatherhood

Once an eagle nested
on the Golis heights
where no camels graze
where no man can
trample the unhatched eggs

The mother sitting on them
waited for the father
to return with his prey from
the Ban Aul plain

And as he returned, she whispered
to him - this afternoon they hatched.
He flew with joy higher and
higher until he could fly no more

Ah! for the first time, fatherhood.

OSLO 16.8.90

A Wish

I wished for a while
I were a student once
again to walk freely
with no burdens and
sorrows.

Just to walk in the rain
just to eat chips or
a slice of bread
an apple or a pear
on a moving train.

OSLO 16.8.90

August Sixteenth 1990

The sunset
and its red beams
are left behind
splendidly visible
for the pleasure
of the eye.

A meteorite fell
from the sky
and burned
the grass, the
diamonds too.

And as the ashes
cooled,
the wind carried
them to the East
to the West.

Fresh grass grew
on the burned ground,
but no diamonds were to be found
on the surface, after
the heavy rain.

OSLO 16.8.90

Flying South

In the morning hours
the wild geese
called waq, waq, waq in
the air.

They passed my window
every day
I knew their destination
was the south.

I wished I could waq,
waq and waq with
them as loudly
as I could and . . .

OSLO 18.8.90

A Loaf of Bread

Like grass mowed
in the spring that
could not bow
to the greeting wind

I walked the streets of
Djibouti not able
to buy a loaf of bread.

I thought what a painful
life for centuries some
humans had led.

OSLO 19.8.90

A Sign

Although you write on
a piece of wood
'don't pluck
the flowers'
and put it up in your garden

It is useless
against the illiterate wind
which cannot read.

OSLO 20.8.90

Uffo I

Uffo is a wind
that comes as
a forerunner before
the rain.

You can smell
it coming
it sweeps through
the land faster
than the light

It carries no chlorine
nor acid rain
it gives happiness
to man and beast.

OSLO 20.8.90

Uffo II

This time the Uffo wind
did not guide the rain.

The sound was
mightier than the
thunder of the heavens

It ignited a spark
on its way through
the land
and as it reached
the injustice house,
it let it loose on the roof
it reached the rooms
and the floor.

The monsoon came
from the Haud and
carried the flame
to the shore.

The monsoon came
again from the north
the flame spread and spread.

The general did not
know what to do
or where to hide
all he could do
was to bomb the towns
from the air
and the ground

But the flame continued
to spread until it reached
the general's door . . .

OSLO 20.8.90

America

The trees that once
bore juicy fruits
are now oozing blood
the earth itself is
torn, the cracks are
visible

I heard your
bullets and bombs falling
on innocent women
and children, I saw how
their blood zigzagged along
the canals under the
citrus-trees,
canals that once
watered them.
The blood reached the
wadi's bed and after
a while dried in the
African sun

And I wished that
it flowed to the
doors of Capitol Hill,
to the doorsteps
of every house,
so that all of you in America
could smell the
stench,
to the White House,
to the Congress steps
so you could see what your
'aid' has done to us.

OSLO 21.9.90

The Teacher and His Daughter

You can't change me
I'm old
and if you try to mend
me
try to mend an acacia
tree!

All you can do is
leave me alone
don't waste your time
telling me to behave
the way you want.

It is too late don't
try again.

OSLO 23.8.90

Expensive Colour

I don't need to travel
to Spain to get my
colour changed,
to use different creams
and endure peeling skin
with all the pain,

Although I know I would
enjoy the gypsy musical
processions.

I don't need to avoid
heaven's rain
to retain the colour
I gained in the heat.

OSLO 23.8.90

A Message with the Wind

The leaves of the birch
are falling now
the streams flowing
quietly through the
woods

The sun is in search
of its dwelling
through the scattered
clouds

And after a season
creeps in and another
crawls out
I feel the first message
of the autumn wind.

OSLO 23.8.90

Written Lines

No purpose do I have
to achieve with the
lines
I now and then write

I don't have to appease
someone I know,
nor change
the planet earth.

I write mostly for the
pleasure of my soul.

OSLO 23.8.90

The Rain-Maker

To God we prayed
with all the begging words
we knew.
The rain-maker climbed
the sacred tree, yet rain
he could not evoke.

The drought continued
to crawl through the
ranges.

The next year we
changed the tree,
the rain-maker too,
hoping God might
send rain down

And the village folk
gathered on the square
waiting for the rain,
yet it never came.

OSLO 23.8.90

The Misanthropes

Beware of those
you help

A dog never bites
the hand that feeds it
so they say

A human will
chop it
off.

Animals appreciate
and cherish the friendship
of man and
since I have known
the rules of their
realm I have realised
that man is
the wickedest
of all.

OSLO 25.8.90

Deep-rooted Sadness

My father died before
I was born, I saw
the light of life and
never saw him once.

The sadness you read
in my eyes
originated in my
mother's womb.

OSLO 26.8.90

Burial Wish

Bury me in the
Qotton plain,
if that is too far
then in the Qolcaday
plain.

Bury me not in
the Haud not
even on the Guban coast
where it
hardly rains.

The death of a good
man is a path
to heaven if he
doesn't stray.

OSLO 26.8.90

No Buzzing Flies

Quiet is the night
the clock has struck
half past four
no hyenas laugh
no jackals howl
no pariah dogs
bark in the dark.

Alas! the crickets
are not out
in the fields
I couldn't
hear the chirping
I used to do
at home.

Ah! at least no
flies buzzing
around my
bed.

OSLO 27.8.90

The Present and the Past
To Crazy Horse and Sitting Bull

One hundred years ago
the Indians
fought the federal
troops at Wounded
Knee.

In the year of 1973
the Indians rose
again and fought,
they preferred to die
an honourable
death like their
ancestors did.

They refused
to submit
to the humiliation
and the disgrace
that for centuries
they had endured.

OSLO 27.8.90

When the Lion Gets Old

Even the smallest candle
can illuminate the darkest
room, and a spark can destroy
a village.

A hurricane can devastate
a mighty land, a million ants
can drag away and consume an elephant.

But when a lion is old,
no zebra can he hunt
nor even a new-born antelope.

OSLO 9.10.92

Flowers and Butterflies
For H.M.W.

Oh take me back to the fields
where we once played, where
in our childhood dreams
we chased and tried to catch
the butterflies.

Where among the flowers
and grass, one hid
and the other sought.

Let us go there once again
and chase the butterflies
pluck some flowers if they are
still there.

Let us see if we can
touch the raindrops
after the rain, on the leaves
of the jujube tree.

OSLO 8.6.93

A Few Steps to Love

Remember how we met
at the edge of the wadi?
You were wearing
that evening a white tobe.

You drove your family flock
to the night shelter
the kraal, before the hyena
came out from its den.

The heart-shaped silver
earrings dangling from
your ears reflecting
the fading sunset beams.

I said 'I love you' after walking
a few steps with you
you covered your face shyly
giggled and walked away.

And I stood there watching
your shadow as it
disappeared behind the
jujube tree.

OSLO 4.4.93

ABDIRAHMAN GAILEH MIRREH was born in Hargeisa in what was then British Somaliland. He spent his early years in Aden, South Yemen, where he attended school and learned English. As a young man in his twenties he spent three years working and studying in Sheffield, England, before going back home to a now independent Somalia. By 1964 he was travelling again to Europe, this time with a scholarship to the University of Leipzig, where he obtained a Master's degree in Agriculture and later a Doctorate in Anthropology. During this period he also spent almost three years working and studying in Norway.

In 1979 Abdirahman left Europe to work in Jeddah, Saudi Arabia until 1982, when he returned to his native country to become involved in farming. In 1988 civil war caused his exile once again, this time in search of asylum. He now lives with his family in Norway. He has previously published three anthologies of poems in English. In preparation is a children's book of fairy tales and fables, some of which are traditional and some his own creation.

Other titles from HAAN include

ANTHROPOLOGY

Understanding Somalia:
guide to culture, history and social institutions
I.M. Lewis

Peoples of the Horn of Africa: Somali, Afar and Saho
I.M. Lewis

LITERATURE

Sharks and Soldiers
Ahmed Omar Askar

A Tree for Poverty: an anthology of Somali poetry and prose
Margaret Laurence

In the Name of Our Fathers: a novel
Abdirazak Y. Osman

'Heellooy': modern poetry and song of Somalis
John Wm. Johnson

HISTORY AND POLITICS

The Road to Zero: Somalia's self-destruction
Mohamed Osman Omar

The Collapse of the Somali State
Abdisalam M. Issa-Salwe

Whatever Happened to Somalia?
John Drysdale

The Struggle for Land in Southern Somalia:
the war behind the war
C. Besteman and L.V. Cassanelli, (Eds.)

HAAN Publishing
P.O. Box 607, London SW16 1EB